The Core

On Values as the real composition of True Leaders

Precious Eda

ISBN 978-93-5610-038-1

Published in India 2022 by Pencil

A brand of
One Point Six Technologies Pvt. Ltd.
123, Building J2, Shram Seva Premises,
Wadala Truck Terminal, Wadala (E)
Mumbai 400037, Maharashtra, INDIA
E connect@thepencilapp.com
W www.thepencilapp.com

Author biography

*** Precious Eda is a leader with a passion for seeing people become better than they already are. He believes in and pursues his life-purpose which is to add value to everyone he meets.

With over 15 years spent in leading young people at various levels, he lives with a commitment towards growing more leaders through teaching leadership and personal development.

A Speaker, Teacher, Mentor to many and a trained Attorney.

*** His series of mini-books on leadership treat singular issues in the very vast subject in each of it's series.

It is designed to make key issues and principles in leadership easy to understand and apply to everyday situations.

***. This work on Values is part of a series of mini-books that treat single points in the very vast topic of leadership in each of it's publications.

*** Other books in the series include :

Vision,Top Squad, How to Beat Your Leader

*** Precious Eda is blessed to share his life with Amarachi Loveth his amazing wife.

CONTENTS

Acknowledgements

“For leaders who dare to be different,

do differently

and make a difference”

Introduction

An Intro to Values

When I watch the TV and read the news on papers and magazines, especially news relating to celebrities and all the gossips and gist that buzz out of the entertainment world, many times I've had to sit back and ponder on a few questions like; why do many entertainers fail to have long lasting success? Why do many of our celebrities die young? Is there a relationship between being popular and spending time in jail? Why can't many celebrities maintain successful families and homes? If you belong to that group that thinks that celebrities are always and should always be in the news especially for what goes on in their private lives, then your answer to the above questions might simply be summarised in one simple phrase: they are celebrities! Or they ought to be in the news.

Well, it is true that they are in the eye of the public and always have public attention wherever they go and in whatever they do, but the fact remains that they too are human beings.

They too have lives like everyone else and simply because they get to live privileged lifestyles don't mean that their lives have to make the headlines always. If you do not have a problem with how their lives play out, I do. My reason is this; as a leader I know that the strongest key available to any leader is influence. Influence is ability to control and exert aspects of your personality on your followers. The people in the entertainment industry and those other celebrities wield a huge baton of influence in our world today, especially over the young generation. They are the most followed on all social media platforms and like I said earlier, their names make the headlines of the biggest news streams. For the very reason that they are leaders, their lives concern me.

If we take pleasure always in seeing all the problematic headlines that burst from their lives every day, we may never know that somehow, we hurt and destroy our own lives. These people stand as role models for millions of young people all over the world, many young people would pay huge sums of money just to attend shows organised by these people or be part of events attended by these celebrities just because of the love they have developed for the celebrities. Young people spend a lot of time on the internet tracking the every move their favourite celebrities make and spend lots of resources trying to get the latest releases from these celebrities. This is influence at its most effective level. When the stories of these public figures are mostly controversial and show how they have to deal with one tragedy or another, or how character failures in their lives are celebrated, the message to the followers is that everybody's life will always have controversy, in fact, your life is incomplete without a sick story coming out of it, character failures are normal because if the world could celebrate huge character failures, then it really doesn't matter if you have a character or if you don't.

I have been in discussions with young people where I heard them argue on which rapper had spent the most time in prison and there was a conclusion that the rapper with the most arrests or prison time was the tightest or "dopest". When people celebrate prison time and arrests, it gives you a clear idea of what the future looks like with the upcoming celebrities. We are destined to have more crazy stories and failures, untimely deaths and fatal illnesses when the younger generation takes over the baton of popularity.

Another interesting aspect of social influence that has caught my attention and I feel is relevant to share here is the sphere of political influence. But on this, though it's a global industry, I'd settle a little bit more in my local environment; the Nigerian situation I mean.

Honestly, from a personal perspective, I must say that it is almost inevitable to lose all hopes on the political leadership of our nation at all levels. Sometime ago I got involved in a heated argument with two friends when one asserted that it is impossible for any Nigerian politician to succeed without belonging to a secret cult or a fraternity. As a Christian, I stood on the side that it was possible to succeed. After that conversation, I had to ponder on the legacy our political leadership will leave for the younger generation taking over.

When you ask the average Nigerian youth what his or her plans are for leadership at any political level, the most recurring answer is that it's an opportunity to benefit from their own share of the "national cake". Hardly does anyone tell you of their plans to serve and make the lot of the people better or to change the cause of the nation. Everyone tells of how when given the opportunity, they would grab it with both hands and change the predicaments of their families. Greed, wickedness, brutally shameless corruption, lies and propagandas, these and many more are the characteristics of our politics in Nigeria. A system that is more lucrative than any other job in the world is just one way to describe our politics. Everyone who joins a political party has one thing in mind and one thing only; to make more money.

So with this kind of thinking, with the painful reality of seeing people with no conscience enjoy so much wealth and store up treasures for generations unborn, the young people have no hope and no positive inspiration to turn to. And those young leaders who lack the strength of character and ability to discern and the meekness to understand true leadership, they live and have one dream and one dream only; to see the day when it would be their turn to loot and spoil the national treasury.

The theme for this volume is values, and it is from all the above that I draw inspiration to write on values in leadership. The bottom line to be drawn after all that has been said is that people have forsaken the emphasis and importance of values in personal development and in leadership.

The idea that you can get whatever you want in life as long as you keep on doing all you can, it doesn't matter what people think or say, it doesn't matter how others feel about you or what happens around you, you can be all that you desire for life if you just stay tough and stay strong on what you do; it is a great idea, and I encourage people to do all of that, but it would be nice if the idea hadn't stopped at that. When people say things like "life is all about the money" "you must never be broke" "money makes the world go round" and so forth… This part of the motivation is the problem, because the idea is that as long as you live never to be broke or just to make enough money for yourself and maybe your family, just keep living. This kind of thinking is the dangerous aspect that undermines the importance of values and there place in human nature. I am a strong believer in the philosophy that without values there cannot be real lasting success. There cannot be a trans-generational success that keeps you relevant even after you have long gone.

In my usual way, I would not attempt to give a strait-jacket definition of the term "values", but I can say that in this sense, I mean with regards to the context of leadership and personal development, values connote morals, standards, ethics, and ideals that are necessary for the attainment of lasting success and reaching goals in ways that appeal to posterity. There was a time when values were the key elements people looked out for when measuring success at every level, but today it really doesn't matter how you reach your dream as long as you have reached it. In this mini-book I try to look at the core values that leaders need to imbibe to attain the success that outlives them. I'm pleased to share my thoughts on what I think are the most important things to do to stand out in our leadership and our personal development even as we all strive for good success.

First

What do Values mean to leaders?

Simply, values are the core of our personalities. They are the distinguishing factors between us and the next person. Values are attached to the cardinal points of our lives. Every person has values hanging over those aspects of living that are important to us. Every person has some values. But most persons never realise that they have values and that's why there is a huge gap of originality in the personalities in our world.

Values are the centre of attraction of our lives to our world. People come close to you or avoid you because of the values you possess or lack. Values define character, and like the famous quote from the movie Kingsman – The Secret Service I'd say here that *"manners maketh man"*. Values are your innermost constructions that consequence on your outermost expressions.

Every word, every action of every man is a direct reflection of the values that shape him. Even God pays more attention to the internal structure of people when He deals with men knowing full well that it is the inward organisation that determines the external appearance.

For groups and organisations, it is the same thing, your people make your company and your company is known by the things your people stand for. It is the values we outline for our groups that distinguish us from others and what we do from what others do. Leaders cannot afford to take lightly the issue of strong values if we desire to ensure lasting success for the things we build. What standards have you incorporated and imbibed in your people? What do the people in your sphere of influence know you for as a company, a group or an organisation? What aspects of your work can be seen as different from the work of others? What things have you put in place to ensure that your people have a success that outlives them?

To every leader, our values mean our lives. We cannot be different from the character we portray. Our present lives are lived in line with our values and our future is shaped by them.

Second

What Values make great leadership?

- **Excellence**

I've read quite a number of materials on excellence, listened to a lot of teachings, seminars and sermons on this topic, and that goes to show how important a topic it is. I would save the definitions of excellence for the quotes section of this work. But to simply put it, excellence is simply doing whatever should be done and doing it well. Yeah, that's what I think, and giving this a second thought, I had to ask myself, how well do many people lead their lives?

How many leaders lead their people well? It is easy to just lead your life normally like every other person does, but that's exactly why you can never be different from the crowd. When you take decisions for your life and your decisions are obviously influenced by the decisions others took for their lives or when you live your life based majorly on public opinions, you will appear like everyone appears. You simply are not living well.

What does it mean to do well?

Of course the mark of an excellent leader is the ability to do things and act in the best ways possible. That to me is what it means to do well; doing the possible best. Nobody wants to do the best but everybody loves to be the best. Every business wants to be the highest profit returner, but not every business owner can do their possible best. Normal and average are the most popular levels of achievement because they are easy to attain. Average is the comfort zone for everyone, and normal is resting point for the populace. But great leaders know that to reach great heights and lead well, you cannot afford to be where everybody is. You can never be remembered for anything if you do something the way everybody does everything.

So…how can we lead well?

Do what everybody does: Yes, that's the starting point; where everybody is, that's where you start. You have to think of what is normal and find out if you are on the same page with the world. The world cannot be moving at a pace and you're being left behind. What are your dreams and goals for your life? Are you pursuing them at the same vantage speed with that of most people with similar dreams and goals? Have you started doing something about your dreams every day? Are your people moving towards the vision consciously? If your answers all seem to be in the negative light and suggest you are behind, then you need to wake up. If your answers all seem to show positivity, then great, the next point is good for you.

Find out what the most successful people do: You've got to search out successful people in your sphere of influence and find out what they do that everybody does not do. People with similar goals and people who lead similar groups or groups with similar objectives as yours. You've got to know what exactly they do that has singled them out as different from the rest of the populace in their sphere of influence. Your excellence can never be noticed if you never try to join the folk of success.

Do what nobody does: Now, even amongst the folks who are succeeding, not everyone dares to be exceptional. Many successful people are always satisfied to be named amongst the few people who are doing a particular thing differently. Not all musicians can win a Grammy, but all musicians wish to be Grammy winners. Very few musicians work towards winning Grammies, and that's why one artiste can have as many as five nominations.

The few are the ones who do what others do not do. But there are those artistes who dare to achieve what no one ever achieves. When someone gets a Grammy every year for ten consecutive years, then you can say that person has dared to go where nobody goes. The greatest Olympian of all time, Michael Phelps has won more gold medals and more medals in total than any other Olympian because he's dared to do what nobody has ever done. When you dare to do what no one does, then you have dared to do excellently, then you have done well.

Do the excellent no matter what: Many times when leaders build a reputation for certain things, after a while of keeping a high standard, there is always the tendency of complacency. Especially when you get to that point that you know everyone will always accept you and what you do because of your reputation for doing well, the temptation to sometimes do any and every how always comes in. But great leaders know that one of the keys to remaining relevant and leaving a legacy is the ability to never lower your standard of excellence for any reason or for anybody. The moment you start considering piping low on this value called excellence, in that moment you begin to lose relevance, your reputation begins to dwindle. It may not have an immediate effect, but slowly and surely, people will begin to look at you with the eyes they use in looking at others. Soon you no longer stand as a point of reference or an example of the best, and when people talk about you, they see you as one of the best. And then if you do not address your falling standard, you soon drop to the normal level where the crowd operates from. That is how you lose your relevance and your leadership grip on your sphere of influence. So to remain at the top, you have to always do the excellent no matter what.

- **Integrity**

In Nigeria, I get really turned off every time I arrive at an event and the organisers fail to start at the time they announced they would start. It's really funny to know that most organisers announce a time different from the time they had planned to start. The excuse they give is that people always come late. But as an organiser, if you always keep to time, people will try to keep up with you. I was speaking to some youth leaders at a seminar and I asked them how they would feel if CNN announced the show Quest Means Business and scheduled it for 10pm and then at 10pm instead of the show, CNN begins to play music videos, and at 10:30pm the anchor Richard Quest appears on screen and starts the show by apologising for starting behind schedule saying that the audience should understand that people always tune in late.

When I asked how people would feel, the whole room burst into laughter. It sounded like a big joke. Well, that's exactly how we behave when we fail to keep to our word. Integrity simply means keeping to your word no matter what happens.

We live in times when there is hardly any truth available to be heard anywhere. Integrity as a value has lost its relevance in today's world because it really isn't necessary anymore. Gone are the days when people do business by first testing veracity before shaking hands. These days, everyone goes into deals with the expectation that the other person is likely to break a promise or backstab at some point. The precautions and cautions are so many these days and you almost feel dissuaded to do anything with someone you don't know. Relationships are supposed to be built on honesty as one of the pillars, but more and more today marriages and friendships are breaking up because there is no trust between people. Interestingly, there is now a difference between a *"correct statement"*and a *"politically correct"*statement. Personally, I think I can recall the last time I heard a true statement from a politician, and I can remember it not because politicians tell the truth very often, but because it was such a rare occurrence.

Is your word your bond?

I once listened to the song *"All at once'*'by *The Fray*, and one of the lines in the chorus was "... *sometimes the hardest thing and the right thing are the same*".

It is so much easier to make a promise than to keep it. Oh yes, I can tell you that over and again. I am a culprit of this flaw of making and breaking promises. Especially when the promises are very small simple promises, I easily forget that I've given my word on something, and most times because the things are very simple, the people I promise often forget too or just decide not to remind me, but the uneasy part is that every time I see them, I always recall the promise I made and then I give an excuse or try to make it up to them. But with experience, I've learnt that things are important no matter how small and simple they may seem. To you who's made the promise they may seem ordinary things for which you merely made a promise you did not intend to fulfil, and you may also think that the people you promise really don't expect you to fulfil them, but to those people, those promises could mean something close to or even more than the whole world to them.

Many leaders never realise that whenever a word is given, a question mark is automatically put on the reputation of the leader. For leaders who care little about values, reputation may mean nothing to them, but for any leader who dreams of giving something more than what the world normally gives and leaving something more than just material things behind, such leaders must consciously give much care to issues that require them to give their words, because in giving their word, they bind themselves with cords that get broken either to build a legacy or to smear a dent of distrust.

Admittedly, one of the hardest values to imbibe in the quest to building a worthy reputation for all leaders is integrity. It's such a hard foundation to dig and difficult structure to erect, but unfortunately, it's so easy to destroy. One failed promise can crash a lifetime of flying high and one simple small lie is big enough a crane with a wrecking ball to pull down a tower. But building integrity with yourself and your people can be easy if you pay attention to and practice some little details consciously on a daily basis.

*** *Always remember someone's watching and listening:*** I bet you, you may doubt this but it is true, believe it or not, people take notice of the things you do and say every time you do and say things. As a leader, it is inevitable to always be watched and noticed. A leader is always on the stage performing while people watch, so it would be foolish to think that as a performer on a big stage, you could do something and it would go totally unnoticed. People will judge you by the things they see you do and hear you say. So the first caution on the road to building integrity is to realise and always remember that someone's always watching and listening, and while you may not be responsible for their understanding the massage you pass, you are indeed responsible for the message you pass and how you pass it.

*** *Before you do it or say it, think it:*** A long time ago I developed a method to check my actions and responses. No matter what anyone says or does to me, I do no reply or react with the first two things that cross my mind. Words are tough and can be even more dangerous than actions, and if are one who has a temper like I do, you would understand that it's difficult to hold back when situations zoom towards you. But as a leader, you do not belong to yourself alone; you're the interest of the people around you and the world. Before talking or acting whether you're happy or angry, give the situation a second thought. Just ask yourself, is this the right thing to say? Will this be the best way to react? If you can do that, you will be pleased with the quality of responses you give in all situations.

*** *Honesty is the best policy:*** Honesty is still the best policy. It doesn't matter what anyone thinks, a lie will always remain a lie and half-truth is never the same thing as the truth. With politics and all the complications in leadership at high levels, it is very difficult for political leaders especially to tell the truth or the whole truth. There's the fear of broken secrecy, destruction of built public image, breach in security, fear of failure and rejection, and all those issues that result when a politician talks. I always advice that to remove all the fears leaders have when they need to address issues especially in public eye, they should try to build a reputation for being honest, curtail how often they talk, respond only when a response is needed and answer only questions you can honestly answer (there's no big deal if you say *"I'm sorry I cannot respond to that question right now"* when you're asked a question that has complicated answers)

*** *Always know that it's not about you:*** When faced with any situation, never forget to remember that it's not about you. Many times we think our safety, comfort or satisfaction are the most important things, we tend to think and consider our personal plight first before doing or saying anything. And then when we say or do regrettable words or acts, we tell people they wouldn't understand because they weren't in our shoes. Of course they wouldn't understand because we never thought about them when we decided to talk or act. If you realise that every word you speak and action you take has a leadership implication, you will always be careful to protect your integrity.

Is it with words alone?

Of course not, and that's why I've been careful to add actions to every of the above points. Integrity comes to play in everything; in how you handle money (especially when it belongs to others), your relationship with the opposite sex, attitude towards time-keeping and things like that. If you're terrible at any of these, you should also apply the guides above to that area in which you experience some hardship. Whenever you have people's money in your possession and there's a temptation to touch it, think twice, remember that people would always ask questions and since you hope to be honest with all your responses, you don't want to be telling the truth of how you used up money that didn't belong to you. If your integrity failure is in managing your relationships with the opposite sex and you seem unable to get a hold on yourself when you relate with an opposite, then the thinking twice really has to be consciously serious. From the moment you begin to receive thoughts that suggest actions in line with your weaknesses, you should counter those thoughts with thoughts that promote questions bothering on the leadership consequence of your actions. In fact, you must anticipate situations that are likely to lure you down and you should respond adequately.

- **Unconditional Love**

Love is my favourite topic. I love to talk about love. Yeah, to me, love is the greatest element to exist in life. Love changes anything and everything. The power of love cannot be over emphasised. No matter how difficult people may seem, an introduction of love to the equation would change everything. For leaders, it is impossible to lead our lives and our people without this value called love. My whole life changed and my perception of others transformed after I read one of my favourite chapters in the Bible - 1 Corinthians 13. It talked about love, and not just love, but unconditional love. I recommend that passage to every leader regardless of whether you believe in God or not, or whether you're a Christian or not. The lessons form that chapter will have a huge influence on your leadership. If you read the words in that chapter and try to fully understand the intent of St. Paul's letter, your approach towards leading your life and your people will turn for a better and more effective phase.

How can love be unconditional?

The conventional line of thought in human relationships is that your response to people should be determined by the way they receive you. If you are accepted easily by people, you find it easy to relate with them. If people are harsh towards you, it's probable that you deal with them harshly. One good turn deserves another. One bad turn also deserves another.

But for a leader, the difficult part of leadership is the ability to respond to people in love regardless of how they see you or treat you. This is more than just showing respect, it is showing love whether or not the other person deserves it. Love is most appreciated when shown to people who least deserve it. When you do good to someone who's been good to you, that's normal, everyone expects you to reciprocate good with good. But when you respond to evil with good, that's

abnormal, no one expects that, and you become a reference point.

I heard the story of a man in America who almost lost his life while trying to rescue school children from a sinking bus that crashed into a river. Some volunteer rescuers lost their lives in trying to save many kids because they dived into the water many times and came out carrying children. After the children had been rescued, there was an interview with this man and they asked him if at the time he dived in to rescue the children he did think of his own children. The man responded by saying that at that moment, all he could think of was the drowning children, his family never crossed his mind. When I heard that statement, I said to myself *"this is leadership"*.

The very ability to forget your own good and give all you can to help another person, someone who you may have never even known. That's true inspirational leadership. Leadership is selfish when it always puts into consideration what there is to gain for the leader first before working for the people. Of course we all hope to get something good in return for the good we do, that's only natural of us, but leadership becomes perverted when we only do good or show favours or go out of our ways to help others with the big expectation of some kind of gain. To put this point more straight forward, we can all relate to a situation where two people are in a relationship, and because one person has some better advantage in aspects of finance and maybe connection, the person with the privileges tends to always do good and make sure the other person has everything he or she requires, provides for all the needs and wants, and all these are done just to ensure that the less privileged in the relationship cannot have an independent choice or reject any proposal. That's manipulation, not leadership.

The scenario looks the same with leadership at all levels. When bosses become extraordinarily nice to a particular member of staff, and always give tips and gifts and let them have breaks and seem to always treat them in more special ways than they do to others, the question that should be asked is, why are they doing all they do? Once leaders begin to show so much care with ulterior motives in mind, they cease to be leaders.

I had an experience with a colleague I once worked with and it was an opportunity for me to understand that really, people find it difficult to trust others even in the light of good actions, and most people are always suspecting when they are shown love and care. We were in a meeting and the meeting had not started so we were still trying to get settled down. I was one of the leaders in charge of organising the meeting so I went around saying hi to everyone one after the other. I got to this colleague and sat next to her and we started chatting up. While we did chat, another lady walked in and she didn't have where to sit. So, being the one responsible for organising the meeting, I quickly got up, said hi to her, gave a good compliment (she looked good that morning), and then we both smiled. I took another chair still close to the other colleague I had been talking with. I was surprised when she said, I was very smart because I did all I did for the other lady so as to flatter her and give the impression that I was interested in something more with her. It took me a long serious discussion to explain to her that what I did was normal and it is expected of all good leaders to show that kind of care for their people, and that it didn't mean I had any ulterior intentions for the lady. That's the way most people think though, and it is because leaders have failed to grow in the discipline of showing care and love to their people unconditionally. It is not possible to please everyone, but it is expected of leaders to as much as they can, treat everyone equally, no matter your preference for any person in your fold, remember the old saying that what is good for the goose, is good for the gander.

Is it just with the leaders?

Yes, I always say that we are all leaders, but at various stages, we are also followers. So the principle does not only apply to leaders in their dealings with followers, followers' relationship with their leaders is also affected. Many times we see followers work for their leaders, go out of their ways for them, give them gifts, volunteer to help them, act as spies for them and do everything just to make their leaders proud. But many times we know that all these things are done merely to twist the hearts of the leaders in their favour. This is also manipulation and not true followership. When all you do in an organisation is first aimed at promoting your personal intentions which most times is to the detriment of the other people in the organisation, what you show is not love, and it's far from being unconditional love. When good things are done regardless of the benefits attached or even unaware of the benefits attached, then we can say that love is being shown unconditionally.

What are the pros of unconditional love?

- **A reputation is built:**When people know you to be one who sticks with the principle of doing good to others without fear or favour, a good name is built and your difference is clear. You are on your way to leaving a legacy in the hearts of people.

- **Good is attracted to good:**It is inevitable for you to experience good, especially when you need it the most, when you show love to people regardless of whether they deserve it or not.

- **Team spirit is strengthened:**Teams always look stronger when they know that the leader depends on everyone and can stick out his neck for anyone. When there is a shadow of favouritism in the team, you can be rest assured that only those who have been favoured will give a hundred percent of their efforts to the achievement of the team goals.

- **A Win-Win situation:**Most times when care is shown by one person who has got some hidden agenda, the other person will always end up on the losing side as they feel forever indebted to the one who's been showing all the care. But when love is unconditional between two people, they both feel comfortable with each other knowing full well that no one is taking advantage of anyone and they can do anything for each other without feeling like they've done too much.

Writing on unconditional love alone would take hundreds of pages, but like we've established from the onset, this work aims at making the issues simple to understand and easy to practice. And that's why I've dedicated one of the volumes in this series to writing on love.

Outro

Conclusion

At the core of every leader's leadership are his or her values. They are the strands that hold every leader's life together. Success or failure lie within that core. Leadership is about people and values give direction to your people-oriented leadership.

If we must build legacies and valuable monuments that would stand the test of time, our lives must be directed by the values that define our core.

There is a story I found to be interesting on the Be An Inspirer website and I'll share it as I saw it:

Lal Bahadur Shastri's Short Story on Honesty

When Lal Bahadur Shastri was serving as the prime minister of India, he went to a textile mill. He requested the owner of the mill to show him some Sarees for his wife.

The owner showed him some exquisite sarees. When Shastri ji asked the price, he found them too expensive. He asked for cheaper sarees. The owner showed him cheaper sarees. But, Shastri ji still found them expensive.

The owner was surprised and told him that he need not worry about the prices as he was the prime minister of India and it would be his privilege to give the sarees to him as gift.

To this Shastri ji replied that he could not accept such expensive gifts and he would only take a saree that he could afford.

The mark of a great leader is the ability to stick to your core relentlesly even the moments when it is most convenient seemingly to violate your personal code of ethics.

The bane of leadership these days is the absence of personal codes of ethics for leaders even at the highest level. When you're at the top, you cannot afford to operate like every other person does. People look up to you. People draw inspiration from you. So you must interrogate yourseelf. What standards do you upohold? What principles are you living by?

Well, these questions can only make sense to leaders who are people-oriented. If your basic desire is to add value to people, then having standards and codes of ethics would always make meaning. The point is, you have to have the right values at the core of your personality.

The present society seems to be the most corrupt that has ever existed. There seems to be an outbreak of unruly behaviours even amongst leaders. But even in the midst of madness people still admire and desire some form of sanity. So, you could see in the United States for instance, Donald Trump became so unpopular because he was perceived to be without the kind of character that befits a President of the US. Recently, in the United Kingdom, the Prime Minister has come under intense scrutiny and many have called for his resignation because of integrity issues in dealing with restriction during the lockdowns of the Corona Virus Pandemic.

No matter how crazy the world seems to be going, people still appreciate examples of quality leadership. It is an innate tendency in man to be good, no matter how crooked people turn out to become, or how rotten a generation may turn up, they would still desire "good leaders". A country may be ranked at the worst points of the corruption perception index, but the people in that country still want saints as leaders.

Recently there have been coups de tat in several countries of Africa and prominent amongst the reasons given by the military for toppling the governments is the failure of the democratically elected leaderships of those countries. When governments drift from being people oriented to selfish ambition seekers, there will be unavoidable failure in leadership.

I chose excellence and integrity as the key values to talk about in this book because they both stand as very solid pillars of successful and effective leadership.

It is easier for leaders with excellent mindsets and integrity at the fore to carry people along. People will admire your work for being excellent and they will trust you for having integrity. These values cannot be negotiated.

Quotes on Values

"Bitter experience has taught us how fundamental our values are and how great the mission they represent"– Jan Peter Balkenende

"One is often so busy doing life that it is easy to avoid evaluating whether you are putting your energy in the direction you value the most"– Deborah Day

"Just as your car runs more smoothly and requires less energy to go faster and farther when the wheels are in perfect alignment, you perform better when your thoughts, feelings, emotions, goals and values are in balance"– Brian Tracy

"Live out your life in truth and justice, tolerant of those who are neither true nor just"– Marcus Aurelius

"Man must feel the earth to know himself and recognise his values. God made life simple. It is man who complicates it"– Charles Lindbergh

"I think the world would be a lot better off if more people were to define themselves in terms of their own standards and values and not what other people said about them"– Hillary Clinton

"When your values are clear to you, making decisions becomes easier"– Roy Disney

To feel more fulfilled, your actions and activities need to be in alignment with what you deem important"– Deborah Day

"You don't get paid for the hour. You get paid for the value you bring to the hour"– Jim Rohn

"If we are to go forward, we must go back and rediscover those precious values – that all reality hinges on moral foundations and that all reality has spiritual control"- Martin Luther King Jr

Other books by the author...

HOW TO BEAT YOUR
LEADER

VISION

TOP SQUAD
PRECIOUS EDA

Precious Eda
#1 Millennial in Leadership

www.ingramcontent.com/pod-product-compliance
Lightning Source LLC
LaVergne TN
LVHW050428160726
843469LV00041B/1274

* 9 7 8 9 3 5 6 1 0 0 3 8 1 *